I
a pot
desire home

I
a pot
desire home

Lal Ded

Songs of the Naked Poet

An Interpretation by
Arvind Gigoo

Om Books International

First published in 2025 by

Om Books International

Corporate & Editorial Office
A-12, Sector 64, Noida 201 301
Uttar Pradesh, India
Phone: +91 120 477 4100
Email: editorial@ombooks.com
Website: www.ombooksinternational.com

Sales Office
107, Ansari Road, Darya Ganj,
New Delhi 110 002, India
Phone: +91 11 4000 9000
Email: sales@ombooks.com
Website: www.ombooks.com

ISBN: 978-93-5376-945-1

Printed in India

10 9 8 7 6 5 4 3 2 1

For Sarla

Sculpting Memory and Time

Translating Lad Ded: My Father's Unfinishable Project

Siddhartha Gigoo

Summer of 1993

The Bhatiyal house
Barrian, Udhampur
J&K State

Pa is back from a long walk. Babi, my grandmother, starts worrying if Pa doesn't return at his usual time. Today, when he returns, he isn't alone. He has brought two labourers with him. A handcart stops outside the gate of the house where we live on rent. Pa instructs the labourers to get started. The two men lift the trunk of a tree and carry it into the lawn. 'Not here. Take it upstairs,' says Pa, pointing to the terrace.

The labourers carry the tree trunk to the makeshift studio Pa has set up on the terrace. It isn't finished yet. Babi and Ma are shocked at the sight of the log being carried upstairs. So far, Babi and Ma have dealt patiently with Pa who has got into the habit of bringing back small pieces from his long walks every day. Branches and twigs and stones. But this time, Pa has brought along half a tree.

'What's next?' they think. 'An entire tree?'

Pa doesn't care to explain. Driftwood is his best friend now. His preferred company, along with his tools—chisels, mallets, hammers, a file, blades, sandpaper, varnish, paint, and paintbrushes. Spending some part of his day in the studio has become a rite.

But Babi isn't angry or upset. She knows it is for her son's good. It is the only thing that keeps Pa from crying, saving him from the depression that had him in its grip last year. So far this sculpting business has worked. Pa doesn't cry much. He doesn't talk much either. It's like he prefers to speak through his creations.

A few shapely models already peek out from the pile of wood. I can't take my eyes off one.

'Is this your first finished work?' I ask Pa.

'Far from being finished, it demands more work…'

'What do we call this piece?'

'How about *An Exile*?'

His body is crooked now. Exile seems to show its effects on him.

'He is all of us,' people say when they look at him. He takes after half a million Kashmiri Pandits who are in exile now.

There's a Christ on the crucifix and a dancer too. Both look unfinished.

*

Every day, Pa goes to the forest to search for driftwood. There are many streams in the forest. Pa spends hours searching for the right pieces. Only he knows what he is looking for. He seldom returns empty handed.

That's how Pa likes to use his time—split between the forest and the studio. It is hard work. Every time he's working in the studio, he has the look of a man possessed.

'What will you do with the tree trunk?' Ma asks him. 'People will take you for a madman.'

He doesn't answer but gives her a soft smile.

Our neighbours, Pa's friends and visitors wonder what to make of all the wood that's found spread in the lawn and on the terrace.

'Everything comes from the streams, the river and the forests,' I say to them.

While he busily works in his studio, they wait for hours to meet him.

They don't know he finds solace in the forest and among the remnants of uprooted trees. They are also for him the saddest of things. We identify with these trees. We share a common bond.

Pa's studio is a cosy place on the terrace. It is meant to store things that need to be discarded. Things of no use—old newspapers, broken utensils, old rugs and worn-out clothes. The Bhatiyals have allowed us almost everything. They are the gentlest of people. 'You can do whatever here,' they say. 'Consider this your own home.'

P.K. Goja, P.L. Goja, Bushan Lal Kaul (known as Dr Bushan Lal), Vijay Zutshi and Arjan Dev Majboor spend their evenings at our place. They smoke and have cups and cups of tea. Sometimes they buy a bottle of whisky.

They often sit in the room with the glass enclosure. It overlooks the lawn. A corner of the room is piled up with driftwood. It looks as if it's a house of wood traders.

Majboor is talking about Kashmir, his village Zainapur and the Standard Restaurant in Anantnag. He is obsessed with Kashmir. Zutshi is a sculptor too. Some of his paintings adorn the walls of his house nearby. *Martand Ruins*, he has titled one such painting.

Majboor recites long passages from *Obra Shech*, his translation of Kalidas's *Meghdootam*. They recite Ghalib, Majaz, Faiz, Hermann Hesse and Lal Ded. He wants Pa to translate his original poems. 'I don't understand many Kashmiri words that you have used in your poems,' Pa says to Majboor.

'I love to use archaic words,' says Majboor.

'Which Kashmiri poet has influenced you?'

'None.'

'Your inspiration?'

'None. I am self-made.'

'You describe nature in most of your exile poems. Where is man?'

'The things in nature symbolise man.'

Pa translates poems of Habba Khatoon and Dina Nath Nadim.

When Moti Lal Saqi comes to our place, he recites a poem on migration, loss and home. He cries.

Majboor recites his long poem *Työl*. The poem is a succession of images. Rhythmic. Musical. A swan flies to Kashmir. It wants to be home one last time.

*

Pa is reading Lal Ded. He recites some vaakhs. Listening to the verses is therapeutic. Each vaakh is striking and teeming with imagery.

Pa visits the terrace less now. Another fascinating obsession is taking its place. He begins his work on translating Lal Ded's vaakhs into English.

The first one—four lines—takes days. Days become weeks and weeks become months.

'Lal Ded is a Zen Master,' says Pa. 'Basho's vision of the world reminds me of her worldview.'

I give Pa a deadline. One year. Deadlines are good. They prevent you from losing interest and Pa is prone to losing interest. He might relapse into depression again, I fear. Last year was terrible. I had thought he would never come out of it. But Lal Dad has shown him a way out of the darkness.

Next year, we decide, we will have his translation published.

*

Almost two dozen notebooks cover Pa's desk. In the course of five years, they've made their home here. A labour of love, Project Lal Ded seems an unending enterprise. Publishing or finishing the work seems to be the least of Pa's considerations.

'Such things can never be finished,' he says. 'The translation can never convey the music, rhythm, passion, philosophy and transparent grace of the original...'

Meanwhile, Pa has translated Majboor's forty Kashmiri poems into English. It takes him months. He goes on refining and polishing them.

He hands over twenty-six poems to Majboor who is running out of patience.

Pa also translates into English Bimla Raina's devotional poetry inspired by Lal Ded's vaakhs.

One by one, Pa's friends shift to Jammu from Udhampur.

Majboor, Santoshi and R.L. Bhat keep talking about Shaivism, Shiv Sutra, Abhinavgupta, Shankaracharya and Osho.

'I have never understood Shaivism,' says Pa. 'But reading Lal Ded is the closest I've come to understanding Shaivism and Zen Buddhism. Lal Ded is a true Shaivite...'

*

'The pot and the potter are one,' says Pa.

In 1973, the School of Buddhist Philosophy in Leh had offered Pa the job of a teacher. Pa taught English to the students there. He also got to discuss literature and philosophy with the Lamas there. After all, both subjects are two shades of life itself. Pa read Buddhist texts. His interest in philosophy soared. He memorised the teaching of the great Zen masters. He recounted stories interspersed with age-old wisdom and knowledge.

In Udhampur, when Pa read and reread Lal Ded, it seemed to me that she was speaking to him like the little Buddha perennially in search of something hard to locate. She was assuming various forms. She took the form of a lump of moist clay on a potter's wheel. She became the potter whose job is to mould the clay and give birth to a pot.

Lal Ded was speaking of the raw earthen pot adrift in rain. She was speaking of emptying herself. She was speaking of becoming the void. She was speaking of entering another void.

She was speaking of losing her way and then finding it only to be faced by the doubt again. *Is this the right way?*

The coming is straight

the return labyrinthine…

She was speaking of pain and pleasure. She was speaking of the master's word.

My body an arc.

The Master's word is fire.

What if the rope in her hand was a sandrope? What can be achieved? She was speaking of the body as the land of exile.

She faced a vast ocean or a river in turbulence. On the other side was home. She was praying for a boat and a boat appeared. How would she cross the river? She prayed for the ferryman. All she had in her hand was a fine thread. She must pull the boat with this fine thread. It wasn't going to be easy. But what if the thread snaps?

Lad Ded was speaking of this pull. Was this the pull of the soul? Or the pull of Home. Or the pull towards Home? Home which is always on the other side of the river. Resplendent and filled with eternal light, where the mysteries of life and the world unravel, where your body, mind and soul become one.

She was speaking of being Home as the only desire.

Truth is a kitchen garden.
Fence it with
reins of white penance.

She was speaking of the Maker as a novice, whose quest too is unquenchable. He is practising, too: the art of perfection, the art of harmony; the harmony that is displayed when all the people, no matter their divergent faiths and beliefs, come to pull the same rope.

That which we are seeking cannot be named. Maybe only her Master knows its name. Unless we burn and pass the test of fire, we will never be able to know its name.

Lal Ded was dancing an eternal dance, wrapped in eternal flames. Her body wasn't bare, she was adorned in golden robes.

The word
a beginning to this naked dance.

She likened candy to hemlock and hemlock to candy. She was saying two is one. Even three and six are one. Everything is one.

…when there is only one

just one and not two

he is seen.

*

Summer of 2023

Jammu—Faridabad

Ma and Pa divide their time between two homes. One in Jammu and the other in Faridabad.

'Do you remember the time when all you did was sculpt and write and translate?' I ask. 'It has been three decades. How is your translation of Lal Ded coming along?' I ask playfully.

During this time, I've read through his work, and I've asked him many questions. Dealing with the symptoms of an ageing mind, he has answered some with words, some with a smile, and some with silence.

Once, in response to my question, he described his interpretation based on how he imagined Lal Ded would have written her vaakhs in English, if she did.

His translation is like the metaphor of the onion Lal Ded herself refers to in her vaakhs; it has layers upon layers that are waiting to be scratched and unpeeled. But to that exercise is attached an element of struggle. It's not easy to get to the core of this creation … the translation and, in the light of philosophical and spiritual discourse, existence.

This creation is layered by the dust of the passage of time, the creative spirit of my father's mind, and the mysticism and esoteric nature unique to Lal's Ded's four-lined, succinct verses.

'It has taken you over thirty years, and your translation still lies incomplete,' I continue to probe him.

Pa smiles.

'Lad Ded's philosophy is eternal. It can take a lifetime, and more, to understand it,' he says. 'My translation will always remain unfinished…'

Translator's Note

While translating the Kashmiri vaakhs (verses) of Lal Ded into English, I found two unequal worlds colliding. I had to resort to inventiveness while making sure that the essence of the original, which is rooted in Kashmir's indigenous mystical and philosophical tradition, is retained, and remains intact to the greatest extent possible. While preserving the densities and complexities of the original verses, I reconstructed their structural, syntactic, and linguistic intricacies. As a result, a narrative frame and a recasting device took shape. You will see that the mythological references of the original remain intact.

In the process, the vaakhs, as they sound in original Kashmiri, lost their punch. A translator is merely a negotiator and mediator between the poet and her readers. For me, this translation is a performance to bridge the distance between two cultures and languages.

Through these shadows, I have tried to give Lal Ded citizenship in another language. I have translated 161 verses from what is available of Lal Ded's 200-plus verses.

Introduction

Lal Ded, also known as Lalla or Lalleshwari, is remembered as the greatest woman saint-poet and spiritual leader of Kashmir. It is said that she was born in Pandrenthan, near Srinagar, between 1301 and 1335, in a Kashmiri Pandit family.

Her years growing up were pervaded by the chaos of a society in flux. Social values were undergoing a change, evolving in the face of the political instability and turmoil that followed the invasions of the land.

That was the time when the last Hindu King, Sahadeva, was overthrown, and Kashmir was invaded by foreign invaders. Lalla grew up in Kashmir under the rule of Shah Mir, a foreign invader from Swat, who founded the Shah Miri dynasty (1339–1561). His mission was to rule and enforce religious conversion.

Orthodoxy was dying and common culture based on Hindu–Muslim unity was shaping itself. Society was struggling for harmony. Through Lal Ded's poetry, we find this process of assimilation manifest on the spiritual plane.

Dissatisfied by society and her personal life, Lalla began to look inwards. What was outside the self was evident. What was inside the self was a matter of search.

Lalla poured her heart in vaakhs. The intensity of her feelings is paradoxically matched by the simplicity of her words. Her language was the language of the masses. However, her poetry is influenced by various philosophies like Vedanta, Shaivism, Buddhism, Vaishnava philosophy and Samkhya, also reflected through the esoteric nature of her vaakhs.

Lalla's early life was full of pain. She was married at the age of twelve to a Kashmiri Pandit who lived in Pampore. In accordance with the customs of the time, her in-laws named her Padmavati. Her mother-in-law was cruel, and Lalla was subject to constant mistreatment and torments by her. It is said that she would starve Lalla but keep a stone in her plate and cover it with a negligible amount of rice to give an impression to others that the plate was full of food. Her husband was gullible and helpless before his own mother and didn't care about his wife. Lalla's father-in-law was helpless too and couldn't do anything though he tried to support her. As a result, Lalla had nobody to turn to for support, succour, and sustenance.

At twenty-six, Lalla underwent spiritual transformation. She renounced worldly life and family and became a devotee of Lord Shiva. She came across Sidh Srikanth, a Shaivite guru, who became her spiritual master. Lalla found solace in his teachings.

Eventually, she renounced all material possessions. She gave up clothes and wandered around naked, reciting verses. She became a wandering preacher, a mystic.

She came to be known as Lal Ded (Mother Lalla). Muslims called her Lalla Arifa. She became a symbol of unity and harmony. She came to be venerated as a great spiritual master capable of influencing even Islamic missionaries and leaders like Sayyid Mir Ali Hamadani, who arrived in Kashmir from Persia.

*

In keeping with the tradition of the times, Lal Ded's verses were passed down orally from generation to generation.

In 1914, a Kashmiri Pandit, Dharam Das Derwesh of Gucch, near Sharda Peeth (now in Pakistan-occupied Kashmir) dictated about 109 of Lalla's verses to Mukund Ram Shastri, a scholar, professional storyteller, and researcher who worked for the government at the time. Shastri then wrote them down and handed the manuscript over to Sir George Grierson. Sir Grierson along with Dr Lionel D. Barnett translated some verses into English with the help of prominent Kashmiri Pandit scholars.

Much about Lal Ded's life is not known beyond what has been communicated orally and documented over the years. Maybe Lalla was a simple girl with dreams and desires but difficult circumstances led her towards spiritual awakening. Regardless, over the centuries, she has come to resemble a symbol of spiritual quest.

Now part of legend, both Muslims and Hindus claim Lalla's legacy and narrate stories to suit their imagination. But if you read her verses, you will see she is not just a poet but also a philosopher and a spiritual master.

*

Lal Ded came to assume even greater significance for Kashmiri Pandits especially after their exodus from Kashmir. Her vaakhs became a beacon of hope and offered the exiles spiritual comfort when they had no one to turn to. Especially while living in camps. They recited the vaakhs, calling upon Lalla to take them home, the *home* Lal Ded longed for. A permanent abode of bliss where there is no suffering and no despair. Where everything is One.

Lal Ded is believed to have died in 1373 in Bijbehara, Kashmir.

1

The ocean turbulent
and
the boat.
The thread thin.
I
and
the pull.
The crossing hard.
I
a pot
desire home.

2

The coming is straight
the return labyrinthine
and
then the evening.
The pocket empty.
The ferryman: Give and cross.
The crossing!
Empty
I am bewildered.

3

The candy load loosens.
My body an arc.
The Master's word is fire.
I am the sheep
without
the shepherd.

4

A wooden bow
but
the arrow a weed.
The Maker is a novice.
In the marketplace
my shop unlocked.
No one knows my craving for the shade.

5

The tear
the sigh
the lamentation
are mine.
Consciousness chained by shadows.
This feast a bubble.
So forgetful of where and what you are!

6

For mind
the other is real
and
mirage is
water
and shadow
is
truth.
Suffer death and birth.

7

Your dance over the pitfall
is
your faith.
You hold on to all
but
then the turn
the exit.
Do you even relish the meal?

8

Five
ten
eleven
baffle me.
They have emptied the pot.
Collect all and pull the only rope.
The cow is lost to all eleven.

9

You are the garden.
Uproot the weeds
and
then take in the daffodils.
Judgement is when you go.
The tax collector
is
behind.
Death!

10

Where did I come from?
Which way will I go?
I am at the crossroads.
Come,
my path
my guide.
False breath is the liar.

11

Coming and going
going and coming
are
day and night
night and day.
The rotation recurrent.
Going home is repetition.
What if
nothing is
nothing is
nothing!

12

Action is living or suffering of others too.
My fruit is my action
like a lotus in mud.
It is mine here
and elsewhere.

13

'Master, name that nothing.'
Exhaustion felled me.
Essence
rose from nothing.

14

Master: 'Shape the rind into pulp.'
'Pardon?'
'Strip!'
The word
a beginning to this naked dance.

15

Sword is happy kingdom.
Closed eyes and alms are heaven.
Master's word is
the sound
the self.
You are the heaven
and hell.

16

Why knot a rope of sand?
The boat will not cross the ocean.
No one can erase the line etched on the stone.
What will be
will be.

17

Truth is a kitchen garden.
Fence it with
reins of white penance.
The fruit of action
is
the animal on altar.
The kitchen garden will be stripped
when
all fruit is eaten.

18

Sloth, hurry, take a brisk walk.
Time to look for the friend.
Fly.
Time to look for the friend.

19

Breathe into fire.
Be a blacksmith.
Alchemy will come true.
Time to look for the friend.

20

I shut the bodied doors and windows.
I caught and gagged the airy thief,
tied him in my hearted room
and
whipped him with the sound.

21

I tamed the horse
and
held my breath.
The moon dripped inside me.
The void entered the void.

22

Are you thirsty?
Hungry too?
Catch the breath
and
you are.

23

The untamed horse saunters
and
is wind in a wink.
Catch it,
tame it,
walk it.
The two wings will control breath.

24

Stamp on the breath,
slit it
bind it.
Body and mind will cease.
And then the metamorphosis.
The philosopher's stone will succeed.
He is the sharp edge of the sword.
Unravel the word.

25

Catch the melting icicle.
Catch the wind.
Put the mound upon
the five.
Cut them
and
see the sun in blackness.

26

Watch the only sound emerge from
the navel
and tie it to the brain and the breath.
Repeat the sound.
The words are useless.
The mind yours.

27

Blew into the fire.
The lamp lit
and
I faced I.
I pushed the light out
and
held it fast in darkness.

28

Endurance is living
lightning
and
thunder.
It is darkness at noon.
It is the I
in a grindstone.
And then
light
lightness
bliss
and
the one.

29

The road became my flesh
my sole.
Only one ushered me into
one.
The listeners should frenzy for the one.
Of the many I heard the one.

30

Hemlock is candy.
No,
candy is hemlock.
Climbing the hill is the gain.
Devotion means reaching the city.

31

The whole of me went to him.
I heard the chime of the bell.
I was stillness.
I knew the void
I knew the light.

32

Do your hands and feet touch blackness?
If your mind Is
you must enter you.
Don't go.
He is in you.
Trust me.

33

Don't free the donkey.
He will ruin their saffron.
Nobody will offer his back
For a sword raised for you.

34

I fell down searching.
Labour outlived the labourer.
My eye beheld the latched door.
Longing hungered to unlatch the door.

35

I burnt the dirt.
I killed the heart.
The result!
'Lalla'
The name spread when I spread my cloth.

36

I was the love-fed tramp.
My days and nights flew by in the search.
The host was the guest.
The find was in the search.
I caught the pure day.

37

The search felled me.
Does one see the walls of the wine-full chalice?
Who can see through the veil?
I reached the tavern when I sank into him.
The goblets are brimful but none takes a sip.

38

The sound doesn't need breath or control.
Desire is not the door.
Reaching the sound is hard even if you are the ocean.

39

The fast, the vow, the paint are no-action.
Fencing your body is no-action.
Polishing the frame is no-action.
Close the eyes.
The sound is the word and the action.

40

The mind on glissade should not be the fear.
The beginning-less is your caring shadow.
It will offer you food.
The sound is the boat.

41

The idol is stone, is temple.
The top and the bottom dovetailed.
What do you name it, empty scholar?
Union of the mind and the breath is the way.

42

He is a florist—the mind.
She is a florist—the longing.
Offer him the flowered emotion.
Wash him with the moon.
The silent word will open His eyes.

43

Grass, flowers, seeds, lamp and water are false.
Master's unspoken word
spoken in the heart,
remembrance through longing and singleness
mean immersion
beatitude
and the final flight.

44

It lids shame, fends off cold, eats grass and drinks water.
The fool drags the animal to the altar for the stone.

45

The pilgrim is on the pilgrimage to see I.
Mind without a path is marsh.
Distance is mirage.
Detach.

46

I am fallen.
Cut my pain even if he is
the trident
or
the flute
or
the dried fruit
or
the beggar's bowl.
What if he is
the first
or
the second
or
the third?

47

Flower is your face.
Stone is your heart.
The word never sank into you.
Wit bled your fingers and wore off your lips.
You are the two.

48

Repetition parched the tongue and the roof.
Action becoming you failed me.
Tired fingers turning beads.
I am two.

49

I removed the watery cloud.
Emptied the ocean.
Cured the sick.
'Listen, you witless fool.
I am.
You are this and that.'
The result: Zilch.

50

You cut hide.
You drive in wedges.
Are you looking for the fruit?
Your seed was no seed.
Word to the unthinking
is
glass bead on dome
is
milking the bull.

51

The unthinking is the caged parrot repeating words.
The recitation is an excuse
a creeper.
I lived the reading.
I live it.
I know it.

52

Reading is a soft pillow.
Action is a sharp blade.
Travelling is a fire and maze.
The word sank in the midst of closed eyes.
I am I because I willed.

53

Reading acted me.
The not-read lost.
The snared lion is the jackal.
First I do.
Then I give.
My knowing is my destination.

54

My diffidence is a latch.
Break it.
When?
When the endurance of
the taunt
the mockery
the sneer
is
the axe.
Erase either/or.
How?
The free horse
tamed
Can do it.

55

Accept and carry vice and virtue.
My ear doesn't hear silence.
My eye doesn't see darkness.
The voiced heart lights the lamp in a whirlwind.

56

Curse me.
Insult me.
Garland me.
There will be no gainers.
I am purity.

57

The spit, the mud, the arrows
My garland
My mirror—
I am
for
my longing is a vine.
When I am,
the garland breaks
the spit, the mud, the arrows
turn nothing.

58

No sting is mine when they shoot arrows.
When I surrender
the mud clears the mirror.
When I surrender
the mud is dew on lotus.

59

Foolery is knowing.
Say: 'Everything is darkness'
when you see.
Unmouth if you hear.
Be an imbecile.
Prattle if they prattle.
Idiocy is the light.
This—
the knower is.

60

Are you painting this body with sensuality?
You are the bin.
Find the king seated on the throne.
He is the charm.
When the gem shines
the shadow and me
change into
a flowered body.

61

Warmth is the answer.
Food too is the answer.
With closed eyes see the spark and the fire.
With closed eyes see the drop and the ocean.
Remember, your body belongs to the crow.

62

My stomach
is
an elephant
is
desire
is
greed
is
energy.
Of the millions, one ran away from the herd.
The result: Light.
Their feet have killed many.

63

Eat and drink
for the body is.
Eat and drink
for the drop is far away from the ocean.
The fast and the mark and the mask stink.
Do the deed
and
the fragrance is.

64

My arrival did not crave for
the soft hay, erect walls.
The lock and the key.
I was not for the warm embrace
and
the rattle of the trinket.
Mine was the barrel and the scales and the mean.
Enough.
I enveloped him
and
the sigh winged away.

65

Feasting is to lose the way.
Fasting is to find the false 'I'
in the shade,
in the cave,
in the mountains.
Cold and hot bring equipoise.
No-exit will become the doorway when you balance.
Not-much-but-less is the ladder.

66

Feast is no peace.
Finery is no peace.
Ladder is no hope.
Scripture is death.
You are you when no hope is.

67

Accept kingship and there is no satiety.
Throw away kingship and there is no satiety.
Death dies when indulgence dies.
Die before death
and
greet immortality.

68

Who dies?
Who is killed?
Who will die?
Who will be killed?
The one who gargles out the word
dies
is killed
will die
will be killed.

69

Master's word and the tamed horse
bring light
bring being
bring deathlessness.
Does one die?
Is one killed?

70

Your name and fame are water in a wicker basket.
Hold the wind in your hand.
Hold the elephant by a strand of hair.
Do it and be.

71

If you stop
the flowing water
cool the flame
walk in the air
milk the wooden cow
you are stuck.
Delusion is the brick.
It is the wall.

72

Killing the robbers
is
serving
is
mastery
is
knowing
is
seeing the dust and the ash.

73

Kill
topping and fire and grip
or
perish.
Offer piety.
Separate 'this' from 'that'.
Be a hawk
and
watch and run.

74

The one is in many.
Find the one.
Accept all and be light.
Stepping upon
wrath and hate and envy
is
the glimpse of His face.

75

Kill
'I desire all'
and
fix your gaze on you in you.
He is expensive.
Fancy is vain.
He is by you.
The traveller is a fool.
The void streams into the void.

76

When you are I
and
I am you
when day is night
and
night is day
when there is only one
just one and not two
he is seen and won.

77

I did not know 'I' and 'he'.
I suffered this cursed 'I'.
'You' is 'I'
and
'I' is 'you'
are the dilemma.
The veil is there.
Who are you?
and
who am I?
The whirlpool.

78

Recite the word in the sun and the moon.
Breathe out the word.
Breathe in the word.
Loosen the grip.
The word will smile.

79

'My home is the hurdle,' said one.
'I will become I in the forest,' said another.
Control the horse wherever you are.
Count breaths in light and darkness.
Then you are you and you will be this.
This is being a record-keeper.

80

If the wheeled time kills my-ness
in the home or in the woods
you are you.
The purity is here and there and everywhere.
Knowing you are you
You need neither less nor more.

81

Lightness, light and knowledge throw you out of the wheel.
The fool tangles knot upon a knot.

82

I lolled fire in lap.
It was death before death.
I was born with no colour, no clan.
Now I am a colour and a clan.
'I am' flew with the wind.
When I was lost I lost the feeling of being lost
and
saw the ocean.

83

Love's hammer
Hammered my heart.
The wicked thief ran away and I was in quietude.
I consumed my seasoned heart
relished the meat.
Will I sink or float?
I do not sink
I will not sink
when I speak
what I hear
what I see.

84

The sun moved the moon.
Before the sun and after the moon
isolated frenzy awoke and sang in pain.
It tamed the mercury.
The kernel sang of the inside of the onion.
I enveloped the pain.
Pain enveloped him.
I screamed:
'Open the door.
I am the wait.'
When the door opened
the ten was washed in marriage.

85

Crawled through six forests and found the silvery disc.
No-breath and no-body killed my-ness.
The roasted heart emerged out of a love ablaze
and
then the pulp
the 'is' and 'isn't' of the onion.

86

In no-time
the dew is frost
the dark is light
the infant is woman.
I, a tramp,
am sod.

87

The river is ocean
Through a spell of lightning
There is no bridge,
there is no ferryman.
The rose is not a rose
not a thorn.

88

In a wink fire is not-fire not-smoke.
The mother in the palace is at the potter's wheel.

89

The sage is hungry like a tree unleafing in the cold.
An unthinking master whips his butler.
I wait for the thread to snap.
I wait for the grip to loosen.

90

You are
a bouquet
a nothing
a curse
dung.
My palm upon palm.

91

One was called.
One caught the river.
One drank with one's gaze stuck to the ceiling.
The pest consumed the ripe fruit.
Ripeness was the termite.

92

The tree is the wife.
The shade lulls.
The stray dog is the wife.
The bite agonizing.
The chameleon is the wife
is change.
'I want light'—
The light is.
'I want shade'—
The shade is.

93

The one asleep is awake.
The one awake is asleep.
The bath defiles one.
The one at home is out of home.

94

The grindstone gyrates.
The handle the confidante.
Motion refines it.
The grains move towards the lower stone circle
then
the upper stone circle.
Search for fineness.

95

The cock crows
and
the lake without mustard waters.
The earthy animals
in a flash
jump into the sea.

96

A flood and another flood and then the third flood.
The recollection is clear.
In one deluge
a throne for me in the sky.
The recollection is clear.
In another a bridge from the crest to the lake.
The recollection is clear.
At last the lake flowed into the void.
It happened seven times.

97

Asleep!
Who?
Awake!
Who?
Which is the lake for its water is dripping?
Which flower is the offering?
Which place is the only place?

98

Mind asleep keeps vigil.
The lake is the five from which drips water.
The 'I' is the water.
Sprinkle.
Super-consciousness is your place.

99

One is the horse.
Second is the saddle.
Third is the stirrup.
The three are one.
The real sees the rider.
Walk on fire.
Walk on the edge of the blade.
The rider is in front.

100

Sound of the word
is all
is void
is everything.
Housed in no-time
in no-space.
Colour?
No.
Group?
No.
Caste?
No.
Form?
No.
Knowing is the image of the sound and the origin.
The sound is the rider.

101

Our being in and coming out
are
mother's pain.
We step back through the door to emerge out of the window.
He is a thorn.
The lesson:
Peel off the onion.

102

The stone
is
the road,
the dais,
the earth,
the grindstone,
the mill.
Therefore,
walk through the hurricane
and
find the grain in the desert.
He is in.

103

She offers the breast and the milk—
my mother.
She offers the breast and the milk—
my companion.
She offers death and the milk—
my illusion.
Therefore,
walk through the tempest
and
find gold in the ocean.
He is in.

104

Everything is the sun.
Water is all.
Empty the ocean.
The spark
was
is
and
will be.
Find him.

105

The hunter has cast the net.
He is all eyes.
Become a prey while the breath is.
The breathless can't be a prey.
Throw off
'I' out of 'I'
and
Face the hunter.

106

He is
the laugh
the sneeze
the cough
the yawn.
He is the daily bath and the nakedness.
He is you.
See.

107

He is all.
Remove the wall.
If you are clever
peel the onion
and
know him.

108

The occult shrinks into a spell.
The spell shrinks into consciousness.
Consciousness melts.
Nothing is in nothing.
The void enters the void.

109

The sun melts into the moon.
The moon melts into the mind.
The mind melts into nothingness.
Time melts into the void.

110

Constance clears
the manifest
the seen
the visible.
Cosmos enters the ether.
Nothingness disappears.
The lesson:
Being is.

111

Word
mind
lineage
can't reach the peak.
The trident and the hairy head are not there.
Beyond these
is
the door
the peak.
The lesson:
Above these
is
the shade
the tree.

112

You and I
the navel and the rope
are not there.
Even he is lost.
It is beyond the three.
The sightless say:
'It is a tail.'
The sighted say:
'All is clear.'

113

Dripping water in freezing cold
turns icicle
turns snow.
Liquid, soft and hard
are
the trinity
are
the
same water
one though three.
The sun breaks one
melts the other
and
gives oneness.
The moving stationary world becomes he.

114

You are life and the earth.
You are the breath of the creation.
You are the sound and the silence.
No one knows your weight.
No one knows.
What?
Your measure!

115

Hear his one
and
lose your one.
The one merged
my one into his one
and
I lost my one.
I am the one.
The war is the two.
His colourlessness dyed me.

116

You are six.
I too am six.
The difference?
You are above your six.
I am under my six.
You are six.
I am sixes.

117

I—
Like cotton—
first bloomed
was spun
and
hung on the loom.

118

I—
Like cloth—
in the washer's hands.
The soap and the beatings
washed me.
He rinsed me.
The tailor's scissors pieced me
Towards the seat.

119

I came from home
sauntered
through the ten.
Am here now.
I
a tempest
cut the void.
He is the all.
I killed
the six
and
the three.
All is he.

120

Threw gold into the fire.
Dirt rose like smoke.
The sun melted my ice-love.
I am the cold.
I am his name.

121

Walked through the void.
The eye did not see the deep space.
When it did
the mud bore a lotus.

122

Delusion and chicane and untruth sank.
I taught the eye and the mind.
He is the man and the animal.
Why not eat and relish?

123

I came straight.
I shall go straight.
I am the straight.
The bent can't bend the straight.
He knows the mouth I come from.
He knows my spring.
What can he do to the straight?

124

Crossed the doorway to the garden
and
entered the deep space.
Saw him and her entwined as one.
Dipped in the undying lake.
Dead and alive
alive and dead.
Why fret?

125

Searched for the inside
outside.
Breath lightened the veins.
With the two closed eyes
and
one eye open
saw the whole as one.
The drop
the spark
the colour
merged with
the ocean
the fire
and
the rainbow.

126

I
a hermit
came and heard the sound with the light.
They will not die when they die.
Who?
Those who are mine.
I too will not die.
For whom?
For none.
Death is a guest.
No-death too is a guest.

127

Want to find his home?
It is at ten plus two.
It is at the bridge of the nose.
Tame the air
and
hear the sound come from
between the throb and the nostril
while breathing in and breathing out.
Kill the image of the image.
He is he.
Who can offer whom?

128

The sky is you.
The earth is you.
The day
the air
the night
the offering
the fragrant wood
the flower
the water
all
you.
You are whole.
You are full.
Who can offer what?

129

First I ran my finger through the hay-ring.
On the ninth day closed the door.
On the tenth day illuminated door number: 10.
On the eleventh day entered the orb.
On the twelfth day joined the disjointed.
On the thirteenth day washed in the one river that was three.
On the fourteenth day controlled the fourteen.
On the fifteenth day saw the moon.
(The moonless days came.)
On the first day the sensual body danced.
Then came the tranquil waters.
This
is
my stone
my idol
my icon.
I am in front.

130

I burnt the body and caught the word.
I ignored the six roads.
I chose the seventh and reached the light.

131

My mind became the word.
I was the speaker and the listener.
I killed the 'I'.
Out of
'that I am'
'that'
alone remained.
And there was the light.
And I reached the light.

132

Cover your body.
Cover my word upon the heart.
The sound became the light of consciousness.
After that death died
and with it birth too.

133

I dusted the mirror.
The mirror was plain.
The dust rose.
He was by me.
He is all.
I
non-I.

134

'Get me the hidden moon,' I cried.
'It is inside,' I shouted
and
roamed outside.
'Get me the like,' I shouted
and
wandered.
'You are the like,' I shouted
and
roamed.
You are the one.
You are one.
The many baffle.

135

When I was I
I lost the ball.
When evening fell
I found the ball.
And I played
the happy play.

136

Consciousness is a flower.
The moon too is a flower.
The whole is fresh water.
My bath
is
my freshness
is
my flower
is
my newness.

137

Action turned into an offering.
Word turned into a spell.
Body turned into knowledge.
This
is
the essence
the dot
the fragrance
and
him.

138

Read the sound
the infinite sound.
Throw the 'I'
and
catch him.
Cremate the 'I'.
It grows into
'Him.'
Non-existence of the 'I'
is
the secret.

139

I the one became I the many.
Embrace lengthened into a distance.
I saw the one go in and out.
I had the meal and the drink.
The thieves left me
hopeless.
They were fifty-four.

140

He is there.
He is here too.
He will not hide in a recess.
He is in the bin as the knower.
He is he—
all himself.
How?
He never died.

141

Everywhere.
Why 'this I'
doesn't embrace
'that I'
when 'this I'
is 'that I'?
Wonder is the lightning.

142

Moving is exhaustion.
Shinning up the gold is exhaustion.
Coming and going is exhaustion.
Slander is exhaustion.

143

Water moved but knew no exhaustion.
The sun shinned up the gold but knew no exhaustion.
The moon came and went but knew no exhaustion.
Man slandered man but knew no exhaustion.

144

The navel is fire.
The head, an icicle.
Cosmos is the flood.
The sigh is hot.
The cold of the head
is
the heat of the navel.

145

I heard the seller shout:
Buy the lotus root.
The wise heard and said:
You want to understand?
Know.

146

Who is father?
Who is mother?
Who is friend?
When you exit
father is not
mother is not
friend is not.
Know.

147

Blackness will rule.
Then the rains.
Whiteness will sink.
All the seven.
Blackness and whiteness
will share the same meal
the same drink.

148

Thieves hide the booty
and
in thirst speak the truth.
They are known for hiding nothing.
Step back.

149

'What is the world for the foolish?'
'A hot frying pan.'
'Who is it known for?'
'The eye, the single eye.'
'Who can know that?'
'Only the eye, the single eye.'

150

Stillness is pepper.
Eat.
Stillness is gold.
Buy.

151

He is the shopkeeper.
'Give me this. Give me that.'
There is no watchman.
Therefore, take all this and all that.

152

The knower of the pain
is
the knower of the pain.
Wearing the garments of grief
wandered
from this door to that door.
They stoned me.

153

The hawk doesn't know the prey of the lioness.
The barren land doesn't know fertility.
The torch doesn't know the lamp.
The fly doesn't know the moth.

154

Get up
woman
and
offer.
If you know
the sound
the threshold
the summit
knock at His door.

155

My decorated house is there in the plains.
It shall remain even when I go.
The shopkeeper has locked the shop and left.

156

I pushed the dark cloud.
I dried the deep.
I cured the incurable.
The fool remains the fool.

157

Do you water nettles?
Do you hatch the viper's egg?
Do you sow seeds in the sand?
Do you oil the cake?
Fool!
Waste!

158

You want to sound the halfwit?
You want to feed the donkey?
Futile!
Fool!
You get what you do.
Don't jump into the well.

159

No sweet juice from the bitter fruit.
No standing for the fallen.
Word to a fool is to itch the elephant.
The bull is indolent.

160

Fragrance doesn't fly from the branch.
The hide doesn't smell camphor.
Your eye on the nose will drive him to you.
The jackal's howl
is
the howl,
will be the howl.

161

For him the spark was heavy and the drink was wrong.
Thirst and hunger were one
when light dispersed to become a cry.
Why drag others to the foot
from the peak?

Special Mention

Uma Shori Gigoo and Omkar Nath Gigoo (mother and father).

Dwarka Nath Gigoo 'Rajkamal' and Savita Raina (uncle and aunt).

Sarla Gigoo (wife).

Amia Gigoo and Aashray Koul (granddaughter and grandson).

Siddhartha Gigoo and Aishwarya Pillai (son and daughter-in-law).

Henna Gigoo-Koul and Rakesh Koul (daughter and son-in-law).

Arjan Dev Majboor, Agnishekhar, and Maharaj Krishen Santoshi (friends).

Pinaki De (cover concept and design)

Shantanu Ray Chaudhuri (editor in chief), Chakrika Pandey (copy editor), and everyone else at Om Books International.